Seeds

from a

Birch

Tree

CLARK STRAND

HYPERION

NEW YORK

Seeds

from a

Birch

Tree

Writing

Haiku

and the.

Spiritual

Journey

Library of Congress Cataloging-in-Publication Data
Strand, Clark
Seeds from a birch tree : writing haiku and the spiritual journey /
Clark Strand.
p.   cm.
Includes bibliographical references.
ISBN 0-7868-6242-4
1. Haiku—History and criticism.   2. Poetics.   3. Nature in
literature.   I. Title.
PL729.S73   1997
809.1'4—dc20   96-25621
CIP

DESIGNED BY DEBORAH KERNER

First Edition
1   3   5   7   9   10   8   6   4   2

for Perdita

Acknowledgments

I could not have written *Seeds from a Birch Tree* without the help and inspiration of a great many people, chief among them my wife, Perdita Finn, whose advice I sought on every matter. It is her book as much as mine. Likewise, the spirit and style of teaching of Eido Tai Shimano Roshi, my Zen teacher for many years, no doubt informs many of these pages. I offer this little book as a gesture of thanks for the pains he took with me. Alfred Marks, translator extraordinaire, offered clarification on several points of haiku which I otherwise would never have understood. In his wisdom and mien, he is the closest thing to an American haiku master I have found. In a similar vein, I am indebted to the works of Makoto Ueda, Janine Beichman, Donald Keene, Kenneth Yasuda, Hiroaki Sato, William J. Higginson, Yagi Kametaro, Harold Henderson and R. H. Blyth, whose translations and critical writings I have found invaluable in forming my own understanding of haiku.

The chapters "Beginner's Mind," "Cockscombs," and "Deh Chun" originally appeared in *Mountain Record*, the journal of the Mountains and Rivers Order. Zen Mountain Monastery, The Convent of St. Helena, Greenhaven Prison, The Juilliard School, Tenafly High School, and The New York Open Center all sponsored workshops at which many of the poems in this book were written.

My special thanks to Frazier Russell of Poets and Writers for funding the majority of my workshops; to the waitresses at the Hungarian Pastry Shop, who allowed me to sit for hours at a café table every day while I thought about this book;

to Michael Sierchio for twenty years of friendship; to the members of New York Haiku-kai, for their continual wisdom, support, and inspiration; to Helen Tworkov and the entire staff of *Tricycle: The Buddhist Review*, all of whom read portions of this manuscript; to my agent Ned Leavitt for his faith in this project; and to Laurie Abkemeier of Hyperion for suggesting valuable additions to the text.

Finally, as always, my deepest gratitude to Deh Chun, compared to whose teaching this book and the others to follow are nothing but daylight stars.

A Note about the Poems

Most of the haiku contained in this book were written by my students, many of whom were writing haiku for the first time. A few, however, were written by authors who are established poets in their own right and whom I wish to thank expressly for permission to use their poems. These are Alfred Marks, Cor van den Heuvel, Jerry Ball, James Kirkup, Ruth Yarrow, and Dave McCroskey.

All poems that appear without attribution are my own.

Contents

Cherry blossoms whirl, leaves fall, and
the wind flits them both along the
ground. We cannot arrest with our
eyes or ears what lies in such things.
Were we to gain mastery over them,
we would find that the life of each
thing had vanished without a trace.

—Matsuo Bashō (1644–1694)
from *Japanese Linked Verse,*
by Earl Miner
© Earl Miner

Introduction

One morning last spring on my way to work I passed a broken flowerpot waiting to be picked up with somebody's garbage. In New York City it's impossible not to notice sometimes what people throw away—what they consider useless or simply old. That morning it was a flowerpot. As I passed it I looked down. There was dirt inside.

My immediate thought was, How could anyone throw dirt away? The dirt wasn't broken; it ought to have been used for something else. But a moment later I had another thought. In the same way that dirt couldn't be broken, it also couldn't be thrown away. Dirt was where everything returned to; it was the *away* to which you threw.

The Bible tells us that when God created man he fashioned him from the dust of the earth, molding his body like clay. Then God blew breath inside that clay and gave it life. That breath is the human spirit—it comes at birth and departs at the end of life. Nevertheless, in my opinion, God's greatest gift to human beings was clay, because with clay came the whole basis for our spiritual life, which consists of realizing our fundamental oneness with all things, our unity with all of nature. For there is nothing that is not included in clay. There is nothing that dust does not embrace.

In a sense *Seeds from a Birch Tree* is about nothing but dust and clay, because all things, including ourselves, have their being in the earth. Take a step in any direction, it surrounds you, it enters into everything you do. But for all that— in form at least—it is also a book about writing *haiku*. For haiku is the one poetic form in all of world literature that concerns itself primarily with nature, the one form of poetry that makes nature a spiritual path.

Haiku began as the opening stanza of a Japanese verse game called *renga*, in which several poets took turns composing "links" in a chain of one hundred verses. The opening verse was called the *hokku*, and the rule was that it be seventeen syllables and include a seasonal theme. Following the hokku, the successive links were made in such a way that it felt somehow inevitable reading from one verse to another in the chain. It wasn't always possible to figure out logically how one verse was related to another, but one could always feel something like an invisible thread running through them. It was my object to link the chapters of *Seeds from a Birch Tree* in a similar way.

If I had to identify the thread that runs through the book, I would have to say that it is sometimes haiku, sometimes the story of my life, and often both at once. For that is the nature of the spiritual path: it happens to someone, somewhere, in a very particular way. Yet, the episodes are not chronological. Often, in retrospect, it was the things that happened at the beginning that seemed most important later on. And if the reader should notice that many of the episodes concern things (events, people, even parts of myself) that seemed insignificant at the time and only later were realized to be essential parts of the path of haiku, then he or she would not be off the mark. In a world where everything is living, nothing can be thrown away. Where would you throw it *to*?

Part 1

The

Way

of

Haiku

The Sketch from Life

Sometimes we look at a scene and after a moment just keep looking, because it is beautiful, or interesting, or sad, or for no reason at all, but just for the sake of looking. Sometimes a moment, just as it is, seems so full of life it must have meaning, even though we may find it difficult to explain. In fact, the moment we try to explain we stop looking, and a little color goes out of the world. Before we know it, the present has become the past and we are somewhere else.

By the end of the nineteenth century, Japanese haiku was on the brink of collapse. Dominated by established schools, each of which claimed to have the definitive rules, haiku had become the province of a literary elite who wrote by formula. Almost no one remembered the poet Bashō's famous admonition, "Do not seek after the sages of the past. Seek what they sought."

Into this era came Masaoka Shiki, a talented young man with ideas of his own and a love of haiku that surpassed anything the nineteenth century poets could have understood. Shiki saw things freshly. In fact, freshness of vision became the guiding principle of his entire literary movement. Within ten years, the established haiku masters were overthrown and a new haiku, based on *shasei* (the sketch from life), had completely revitalized the art.

Shasei stressed direct observation in the manner of a landscape painter who carries his sketchbook to the field and draws exactly what he sees. More than realism, however, the sketch from life offered Shiki and his followers a way of seeing nature as though for the very first time.

In America, as we come to the end of the

20th century, it is questionable whether we ever really see nature at all. Most of us live our lives behind walls. We drive nearly everywhere we go. We work in temperature-controlled environments. When snow falls, we salt our driveways to melt it right away. Few if any of us know the names of more than twenty birds or flowers.

Because we have forgotten nature, there is a feeling of loss at the heart of modern people. We try to fill the inner lack with wealth and power, or with distraction, but this does no good at all. Each age has its own unique sadness. This, it seems to me, must be our own. Is it any wonder we have lost the meaning of our lives?

The Way of Haiku is to return to nature. We accomplish this by letting nature back into our lives. As haiku poets, we begin simply, by carrying a notebook and walking in nature every day. Then, gradually, we learn to sketch from life. At the end of each notebook I fill with haiku, I am always struck by how much more of the world I have seen, and how much more in love with life I have become.

Back
from
the
Mountains

From the time I was a young child I enjoyed long solitary walks. I felt overwhelmed by the beauty of nature—a kind of mute wonder at the beginning of every autumn when the leaves changed color and began falling from the branches. In springtime I struggled with the feeling that there was a language in the blossoming of trees. As the years passed, those feelings remained inside of me, growing layer upon layer with every passing season.

One afternoon in early springtime, when I had been playing tennis all day, my high school girlfriend arrived in the bleachers with a small flat package which she held on her lap until the match was over. The package contained a book of haiku which she offered to me saying, "These reminded me of you." And so I unwrapped the package and opened the book to the following haiku by the Japanese poet Issa:

Beginning of spring—
the perfect simplicity
of a yellow sky

It was late in the day. The tennis courts were on a hill, so when I looked up I could see the sky extending far into the distance beyond the river. It was just as Issa said: a yellow sky. That is how a haiku works—in seventeen syllables, the poet captures a moment from the life of nature.

After reading the poem by Issa I was hooked. I continued to write other kinds of poetry for some years, but gradually I came to write only haiku—every day, every place I went. If I went into the woods, haiku went with me. If I woke in the middle of the night to find that my foot had come out from under the covers, a haiku would form in my mind. Perhaps I should have realized that that was enough. But I was not content. I felt a spiritual longing that would not be satisfied with staying where I was.

I took up the study of Zen Buddhism, first informally, with a Chinese hermit who taught only by example, and then later according to the traditional model of Japanese Zen. During those years, I frequently meditated through the night. When that was not enough, I organized a small group of Zen practitioners who were willing to meditate all weekend once a month. But finally that too proved insufficient, so I left my wife, went to live in a Zen monastery, and eventually became a monk.

The monastery schedule was rigorous: endless hours of meditation, silent meals eaten with chopsticks from lacquer bowls, and hard manual labor over rough mountain terrain. And there was the persistent demand by the abbot that I pass my *koan*, or Zen riddle.

I took the matter seriously, following the advice of one ancient master to carry the koan with me night and day. Altogether, in and out of the monastery, I did this for twelve years, during which time many other students passed their first koan and began to work through the traditional curriculum of several hundred others. Finally, when I had given up, the answer came. But I no longer cared that I had passed it, and when my teacher presented me with the next in the series of traditional koans, I had to resist the sudden impulse to laugh. I knew nothing. The journey had doubled back to where it started. And so I left.

At first I did not know what to do. I had given up everything to become a monk. I even gave up haiku because it seemed like a distraction from my spiritual life. When I finally also gave up the monkhood, it seemed as though there was nothing left. I had devoted my adult life to the study of Zen, and now it seemed that I had stepped unexpectedly out the other side to find myself in an unfamiliar land. There was an enormous vacuum in my life.

But gradually something started to happen. It seemed like nothing at first. I simply began taking long daily walks to lose myself in nature, and slowly I began writing haiku once again.

My true practice had always been writing haiku, but it took many years in the interim to rediscover the simplicity of that. Haiku is not an ideology. That is the essence of haiku art. Because haiku demands a fresh creative response to each new situation, and because it places images before ideas, it is guarded from becoming a religion. Rather, haiku is a spiritual path.

back from the mountains
a yellow handrail guides me
down the subway stairs

Beginner's Mind

One day a visitor asked Sen no Rikyu to explain the secret of performing the Japanese tea ceremony. Rikyu answered: "In summer suggest coolness, in winter a feeling of warmth. Lay the charcoal so that it heats the water, and make a pleasing bowl of tea. That is all." The guest was disappointed, however, and complained, "But everyone knows that." Rikyu only replied, "Serve tea in this way and perhaps I will become your student."

As technical instruction Rikyu's words are a disappointment. Their spirit, however, suggests a mind which is simple, straightforward, and clear. It is the mind of a man who, having mastered his art, has given up that mastery in order to become like a beginner again.

A haiku is a seventeen-syllable poem about the season. Arranged in three lines of five, seven, and five syllables, and balanced on a pause, a haiku presents one event from life happening now. However much we may say about haiku, its history or its various schools, it is difficult to go beyond these three simple rules: form, season, and present mind. Even a lifetime of practice cannot exhaust them, and we may sometimes find they are difficult to follow even after twenty or thirty years.

Despite the subtlety of these guidelines, I have often found that when I give workshops and retreats at least one of the participants is able to write a haiku as good as any I have seen. When this happens, everyone is moved. Even those whose efforts have been less successful feel as though something has happened to them. We could say in such cases that everyone has been served "a pleasing bowl of tea." Some weeks or months later, however, the author will say, "I haven't been able to write another haiku—at least not as good as the one I wrote before." When this happens, my advice is always the same: "Don't worry about success. Just return to the beginning, and see what happens."

In the year before he died, the Japanese poet Matsuo Bashō wrote the following verse:

Chrysanthemums bloom
in a gap between the stones
of a stonecutter's yard

A Japanese critic once said that a poem like this, which is plain but evocative, can be written only by a total amateur or a great master.

As beginners, we may feel some confusion when we read a statement such as this. How could a poem by Bashō, often called the greatest haiku master, have just as easily been composed by a complete amateur? We want beginners to be awkward and masters to be great. But at the end of his life Bashō wrote this very fresh "beginner's poem" about something he saw. This is rather extraordinary. It may run counter to our expectations about mastery, but it illustrates the fundamental point about the Haiku Mind: it is available right from the start of practice. In fact, it may be more available to the beginner than to the person who has been practicing for some time.

The more we learn about haiku, the more we may be tempted to think of ourselves as experts. If we go too far in that direction, however, our poems will lose their freshness. What was once as simple as looking at chrysanthemums blooming in a gap between stones will have become an intellectual exercise. For this reason it is far better to retain the wakeful, open mind of a beginner than to accumulate mere knowledge about technique. Rikyu understood this point, and so did Bashō. Though both men were well-educated and understood all the intricacies of their art, each held first to the value of a clear, open mind, even at the end of life.

Seasonal, direct, and clear, the haiku form itself expresses the fundamental truth about human life. Our appreciation of this truth grows only deeper as we follow the passing of every season. Therefore, although the seventeen-syllable haiku

is very brief (only the length of a breath), its practice may last a lifetime.

> Adirondack rain:
> walking barefoot over rocks
> and little mushrooms

Caterpillar's Web

Caterpillar's web—
invisible to passers
caught in its weak trap

—Peer Casillo

The caterpillar's web is actually only a single weak thread. In late May in the northeastern United States many thousands of these small creatures (called inchworms by most people) lower themselves down indiscriminately from the branches. Only someone who is not in a hurry will notice the tiny green body suspended below a shade tree. Others walk right through, unaware of the small claim laid upon them by a thread.

This poem was written by a 14-year-old high school student from Tenafly, New Jersey. It was his first haiku.

Counting Syllables

The place to begin is counting syllables—five-seven-five. At this point the mathematician and the child are about on par. If anything, the child may be better at counting naturally, and with presence of mind.

If we take up Zen meditation, we will be given the practice of counting our breaths from one to ten, coming back to one whenever we lose count. When we reach ten, we begin again. Anyone who has tried this for any length of time will know how often various thoughts and worries interfere with this simple task. But in time we learn to count, something we always thought we knew but in fact performed only by rote. Performed artlessly, but with complete presence of mind, counting becomes an expression of sincerity. It promotes the kind of humility that becomes the basis for a clear, straightforward vision of the world. Both in meditation and in haiku, counting must become a very present, wholehearted activity.

When we practice meditation, we begin by sitting cross-legged on the floor with our buttocks firmly supported by a cushion. Next we erect our spine and sway gently back and forth to find the proper point of balance. Once we have settled down, the ears will be on line with the shoulders, and the navel with the nose. The eyes remain half-open, gazing at a space before us on the floor. Left over right, the hands form a relaxed but clear-looking oval, resting palms up in our laps. And the tips of the thumbs just touch.

When we look at someone sitting in this way, they seem attentive, but very calm. We may think of them as beautiful or even wise. It is for this reason that even people who do not practice

Zen, or any form of Buddhism, often have Buddha statues in their homes—to remind them of the serenity found in simple forms.

Of course, even people who do not practice Zen can write haiku, for pleasure or even as a spiritual path. Like Zen, haiku has its own form and specific guidelines for practice. But people frequently do both Zen and haiku and find that they complement each other in a natural way. Haiku may complement other spiritual paths as well.

If we have no interest in using haiku as a spiritual practice, it is unnecessary to count syllables at all. We could, for instance, write a haiku in any form—one line, four, or seventeen—and include the season or not as we pleased. But I doubt we could take much long-term satisfaction from this kind of haiku. I doubt if haiku would endure beyond a few decades in America if it were practiced in this way.

Because haiku is so subtle, it is necessary to have some definite form. Otherwise, beginners will have no place to start, and experts will soon forget their beginner's mind in the obsession over where to break a line. Already there are too many experts of this kind.

There is a mistaken belief that form is confining and limiting. In reality, nothing has done more to limit the development of haiku in English than this idea. Ultimately, it is the very strictness of haiku which allows us to *forget* the form and enter into a more profound relationship with nature and other people. Once forgotten in this way, the form becomes unbelievably playful and light. When the form remains unfixed, however, then poets become stuck at the level of form. Paradoxically, by rejecting it, they become its captive.

Counting is a universal practice. Its humble, straightforward vision of man and nature is at the core of all human experience. However far we may stray from it, everything comes back to this.

rain at the window—
how many more ants before
the end of summer?

Reading
a Haiku

A paulownia leaf
caught all the while in sunlight
flutters to the ground.

—Takahama Kyoshi
(trans. by Donald Keene)

The Japanese poet Takahama Kyoshi is said to have claimed that, for him, this verse expressed all the wonder of heaven and earth. The American scholar Donald Keene suggests, however, that it would take an exceptionally sensitive reader to discover such dimensions in the poem. I do not agree. You can discover these dimensions for yourself. This is how.

Repeat the poem several times out loud, until you are able to recite it without looking at the page. Feel the sound and rhythm of the words. In this case the poem is a translation—but a good one, so you should be able to get some of the feeling of Kyoshi's original poem. When you are able to recite the poem from memory, keep saying it silently to yourself as you begin to imagine the scene. Watch the leaf as it comes loose from the branch. Watch how vividly it flutters in the sunlight on its way to the ground. Don't hurry. Allow the imaginary leaf to make every revolution as it falls. Keep watching it until it comes to rest, still sunlit, lying upon the ground.

When you have practiced reading in this way for a while, you will begin to discover that you are able to experience many different layers in the sound and texture of a poem. A single haiku then becomes a journey.

Keene said it would take an exceptionally sensitive reader to discover the layers of Kyoshi's poem. In reality, it only takes a poet. You can become a poet if you practice reading haiku in this way.

hot rock by the stream
each of the baby's toeprints
evaporating

                    —Ruth Yarrow

Swim Beach at low tide:
a fragment of blue sea glass
with the rocks & shells

                    —Susan Rudnick

the cat fluffs his fur
and tries to avoid the cold
of his own shadow

                    —Perdita Finn

dew covered shore stones
all the way down to the lake
and under water

—Dennis Davidson

weather beaten boots—
little steel clips reflect light
that warms the sharp air

—Sharon Lee

The Four Seasons

Nearly every haiku contains a *kigo*, or "season word." From the beginning the purpose of haiku was to evoke a seasonal feeling—the kind of feeling you get from watching leaves fall in autumn or from waking to the sight of freshly fallen snow. A haiku uses a season word in conjunction with another image or phrase to record such feelings and to evoke them in the reader's mind.

But what exactly is seasonal feeling? The phenomenon is too rich and varied to ever fully define it, but one helpful way of looking at it is to realize that seasonal feeling always has two aspects: the fleetingness of life and the eternal harmony of the natural world—in other words, the passing seasons. Seasonal feeling, then, is a way of realizing that all things come into being, have their lives, and pass away within the larger context of nature—something so vast and all-inclusive we could never see it whole.

In haiku, the use of words belonging to a certain season allows us to evoke the whole of nature by referring to one particular thing. For that reason, you might say that the season word functions as an anchor—a point of connection with the natural world.

"The things of nature," wrote Kenneth Yasuda, "are born and fade away in the rhythm of the seasons." The same holds true for humankind and all its works. Thus, when we look at nature, we are looking at something of which we are a part. Being human, we can stand aside and consider, for instance, what images we want to use to form a poem. But those images, like our lives, are meaningful only as they stand in relationship to nature. The themes of haiku recognize this truth. We are one with nature. How could it be any other way?

Clear
Water

Once when I was giving a workshop at Greenhaven prison, an inmate told me that it was difficult to write haiku there because there was no experience of the season. We were sitting in a bare room with a concrete floor in which, twice a week, the prisoners did formal Zen meditation.

The heat was stifling. A large industrial-sized fan churned the slack out of the air and dumped it in the far corner of the room where it quickly resumed its torpor. A single fly, himself a prisoner, made wobbly circles through the room, almost driven mad by the heat. "It's too bad you're locked up in here," I answered. "But you can't fence nature out. It's all around you, in everything you do." I wasn't sure whether or not they were convinced, but after lunch one of the men handed me this poem.

from the jailhouse sink
the water comes out so clear
I feel cool by it

—Jakko Medina

Taking a Haiku Walk

I have found that it is best to approach haiku in simple terms. Respond to what lies directly before your eyes, and choose your words in a relaxed and open way.

In its simplest form, writing a haiku is closer to collecting shells than searching for the proper word. When you go to the shore to collect shells, you just walk along in a relaxed way, now and then stooping down to look at something interesting or beautiful. Sometimes you pick up a fragment for its shape or color, and sometimes a fully formed shell. If you take a daily haiku walk in this same spirit, soon you will find that haiku come all by themselves.

For many years I used to take a one or two hour walk each day for the purpose of writing haiku. That was my daily practice. However, it took quite some time before I was able to learn to approach these walks in a haiku way.

Matsuo Bashō once wrote, "There is one thing which flows through all great art, and that is a mind to follow nature, and return to nature." Since Bashō's day, those words have often been used to explain what is meant by the term "haiku spirit" or "haiku mind." But how many people really look at nature? How many people really notice nature and take what they notice to heart?

Some years ago I worked on Wall Street as a proofreader for a corporate law firm. Each morning I would ride the subway downtown to lower Manhattan, where I would work in an office without windows throughout the day. During lunch I would always go outside. Only fifty yards away was Trinity Church. From the churchyard it was possible to see the sky. Often sparrows would come to eat the leftover crust from my sandwich, and in the summertime there were bees and sometimes butterflies. Once I saw a large green dragonfly accompanying a stream of men in dark business suits as they passed by on the sidewalk. The dragonfly hovered just above their heads.

One day I was waiting in the downstairs lobby of my building to meet a friend for lunch. It was raining and my friend was late. With nothing else to do, I stood behind the plate-glass doorway and watched people passing in the rain. From where I stood I could see the entrance to the New York Stock Exchange across the street.

As I waited, I noticed people going and coming through that door. Before they entered, the men in tan raincoats would all hunch their shoulders together when closing their umbrellas. I remember this because I had never noticed it before. Probably everyone closed their umbrella like that on a rainy autumn day.

As I continued watching, however, I noticed that many of those leaving the building (they were mostly men) didn't notice the rain. Had it been raining really hard, they would have. But because these were the single raindrops of early autumn, it didn't register right away. After taking a few steps, however, invariably they would glance up at the sky, turn back into the building and emerge a few moments later with an umbrella, or a coat and hat. All except one man.

One man didn't notice anything at all. He left the building without an umbrella or a raincoat. He wasn't even wearing a hat. As I watched, he walked the length of the block toward Broadway, rounded the corner and was gone. I waited a few moments, staring in the direction he had gone, but he didn't reappear.

Years later the thought of that man is still with me. Sometimes I imagine that when he turned the corner he stepped immediately into the lobby of another building, that he had been going only a short distance and had simply thought to himself, "What's a little rain?" But I have to admit that his manner of walking gave no indication that he noticed the rain at all.

Compared to people only a century ago, we are almost all like this. The rhythms of nature are the same, but the world we have constructed for ourselves does not always account for nature. Nature occupies a small place in our lives, if and when we really notice it at all.

I have found that in writing haiku, I have gradually been able to let nature back in. In the beginning I saw haiku as an opportunity for making a very special kind of poetic art. Later I used it as a kind of discipline. Now haiku has become like the land itself. Each morning when I wake up I wonder what kinds of things I will notice as I walk the boundaries of that land.

loving its whiteness
I walk around the birch tree
to the other side

• Try This •

Take a thirty-minute walk. Dress to suit the weather, and carry a notebook.

- In the first ten minutes, keep your notebook in your pocket. Just relax into the feeling of being outdoors. Notice the weather and any plants or animals you come across, but keep walking. Let your body loosen and relax.

- In the second ten minutes, let nature begin to displace the ordinary day to day concerns that occupy your mind. Take the time to pause briefly over things that strike you as beautiful or interesting in some way. Such pauses create a space in your life for something to enter in.

• In the last ten minutes, let that *something* come in. Now take your notebook out of your pocket and carry it in your hand. The space you created in your life a few minutes ago now becomes the space to write a poem.

For the purpose of this exercise, you may walk out and back from home. Or you may walk to some separate destination. But whichever you do, make sure that your purpose is only to walk, to be outside in nature, and not to get somewhere. Not even to write haiku.

After you have practiced this exercise for a while, you will find that you don't need to structure your walks anymore. Having relaxed into nature and momentarily set your other thoughts aside, you will know for yourself the proper moment to write a haiku.

Mountain
Laurel

the mountain laurel
hasn't turned, but every leaf
is notched or bitten

—Carl Sherman

This haiku was written at a workshop in the
Catskill Mountains. That weekend the weather
had become increasingly cold. The leaves were
past their color, and only acorns were still falling

from the trees. Once we reached our destination, I gave a talk about composing from nature. Few of the participants had written haiku before, so I kept it brief, telling them only to look carefully and find whatever they could. The group fanned out over the mountainside, and I walked from person to person, answering questions until it seemed that everyone had the proper feel.

I had hiked Mt. Tremper before, so I went somewhat farther than the others. I remember noticing how the coolness crept further inside my sweater as I climbed. Finally, I came over the top of a ridge and saw a solid wall of green before me, about fifty yards distant. It was disorienting. Then, after a moment, I realized it must be mountain laurel.

When I crossed back over the ridge, I met up with a member of the group. He seemed comfortable walking alone, so I suggested that he try going further north and pointed in that direction. Later, I was pleased to see the haiku he had written. But I wasn't surprised—there had been a haiku there already, waiting for someone to come.

Haiku Diary

From my own experience, I have found it helpful to keep a moderately messy notebook— one in which I can feel free to scribble notes at random moments of the day. If you regularly carry a backpack or a shoulder bag, this may be of standard size—otherwise, somewhat smaller. The notebook should be neither cumbersome nor tiny. Use a blank book that does not have the dates already printed in it. You will not know beforehand how much or how little you will write on a given day, if at all.

The correct way to use the haiku diary is just to be very free and open. Don't set a single format. Don't organize the book five haiku to a page or limit it to poems and dates, excluding prose. You may even find that you jot down an occasional phone number or appointment in its pages when no other book is handy, or—if you are an artist—a sketch of some interesting scene.

Write down your haiku just as they come to mind, without too much deliberation over whether they are good or bad. Improvement takes place slowly, so set them down the way they come and stay alert for the next opportunity to write.

When I describe the haiku diary in this way, people sometimes get the mistaken impression that they ought to relax or even ignore the rules of haiku. This is not the case. If one wants to use poetry as a spiritual practice, first one has to be a poet; otherwise, it is all a sham. The important thing to remember in keeping a haiku diary is this: each time you write, make an honest effort to compose a poem in the proper form. Make this effort every time, whether you are successful or not.

Bashō once said that anyone who had written five haiku during his or her lifetime was a poet, whereas the person who wrote ten or fifteen was a master. Some poets interpret this to mean that Bashō set his standards very high. I think his real intention was to defeat the acquisitional attitude of mind that afflicts so many poets.

For seventeen years I kept a notebook in which I recorded my best poems from each haiku diary. Every few months, I would transfer them into the book and throw the diary away. Then, one day I came home from a walk having written my first real haiku. So that night I took my precious notebook out on the back porch and burned it, without even looking at any of the poems. I simply knew that no amount or ingenuity or craft alone can make a haiku.

Where Haiku Come From

To begin with, I think we could say that haiku come from real events. But that is not entirely right, because the event itself will not make a poem, much less a haiku. The Japanese author Yagi Kametaro wrote, "To the single image the poet's mind must add a turn of thought; the poet's mind is crucial." In other words, the poet cannot be merely passive. For all its realism and objectivity, a haiku is not a photograph, but a poem.

Ultimately, where haiku come from is a

mystery. Some haiku result from imagination. Some idea or feeling catches our interest, and we begin to imagine a phrase or image to match it with. This method of composition rarely results in great haiku, but even when the result is acceptable, we are still left saying that the poem came out of imagination, which is to say ... it's rather mysterious after all.

Once we begin to speak of haiku as a spiritual practice, where haiku come from becomes at least a more familiar mystery. Engaged in some activity—walking, for instance, or working in the garden—at a certain point a haiku just comes right out of that activity as its natural expression. It may be something we have seen or heard, a momentary reflection, or a phrase that slips right out in conversation.

One day last summer I took a walk along Buzzards Bay with my father-in-law, Matt Finn. At one point he stopped beside a tidal pool and made the remark, "When the tide goes out all the minnows leave the pool." Then, a moment later, he added, "I've been looking at that all my life." On the way back to the house, we passed the pool again, and it was just as he had said—the minnows were all gone. A moment after that, I realized that Matt had composed the first two lines of a haiku, so I added a third from what struck me about the scene.

when the tide goes out
all the minnows leave the pool—
it's cloudy weather

So, one way of looking at it is to say that we go to a particular place and write the poetry of that place. We simply describe in seventeen syllables what we have seen—what struck us, or moved our hearts. So, although it is still a mystery, when someone asks where a particular haiku "came from," we can at least offer a particular place and time.

The
Salamander

on a creekbed rock
a salamander resting;
its tail in water

—Emi Stanley

A very fresh haiku, slightly cool—the kind
of feeling one gets from holding up a finger to
test the wind.

The poem has an interesting history which

the poet shared with me a few months after the workshop where it was written. According to Emi, she had looked in vain for a haiku that day. Finally, when she had almost given up, she recalled a nearby place some children had shown her a few months before.

The children had said, "You wanna see someplace secret?" and Emi said yes. They led her to the far end of a tunnel where a stream came out after running underneath the road. Several months later, Emi thought that she might have better luck finding a haiku in the place where the children had led her. So she went there and sat down on a rock looking at the stream. And waited.

After a few minutes a small red salamander came to rest before her on a stone. After she told me this story I felt I had a much deeper, if simpler, understanding of something Bashō had once said. When asked the meaning of "lightness," he replied, "Just observe what children do."

The Group

Like any spiritual practice, haiku is something that happens in a group. However, if that group becomes a thing in itself, then its spiritual aspect will be lost. So in haiku we keep things small.

Most haiku groups are composed of six to ten people who meet once a month to share their poems. At such meetings each poet submits anonymously three or four haiku on separate index cards. These poems are shuffled and read aloud, and each poet chooses the five haiku he or she likes the best and explains why. The poem that receives the most votes is declared the winner, which simply means it is the kind of haiku that the group prefers.

Haiku is unique in the world of poetry, and there is no mystery as to why haiku has evolved as a kind of group art. Unlike longer poems, a haiku can be grasped all at once. In fact, haiku could almost be defined that way. When we read a haiku through to the end, and then touch back briefly on the beginning to get the moment whole, an image forms in the mind. The effect of that image is to show us what the poet saw, what inspired him to compose a poem. And that evokes a smile. Thus, haiku is all about sharing. Everyone in the group is a poet; everyone is a reader of poems.

What we share in haiku is a feeling for the season—for the longness or shortness of the day, the angle of the sunlight coming through the trees, the shape and altitude of the clouds—all the things which change with the season, coming into being and vanishing before our eyes. As haiku poets we observe and appreciate these things together as a group. Sharing those experiences deepens them and deepens our relationships to one another. The result is that we become more present, more profoundly connected to where we are.

The members of a haiku group therefore are all people who live close to one another. Although they may sometimes submit poems for publication at the regional or national level, the focus of all their activity is local. In my experience, this is what makes for the deepest and most lasting spiritual life.

A Gift

When I first began seriously writing haiku, I was a member of a group. Not a haiku group, but a ragtag group of college students with an interest in Zen. We held *zazen* meetings every morning in the drafty little house we rented from our studio art professor, shared meals together, and read the same books. There were three of us to begin with: Steven, Michael, and myself. Later Steve's girlfriend Lucy moved in.

It all started like this. I had begun meditating in the fall of 1977, when I left school abruptly at midsemester to travel to International Dai Bosatsu Zendo, a traditional Japanese-style Zen monastery that had opened in the Catskills the year before. There I was offered the briefest instruction I have ever received. "Sit," was all the abbot said, and lowered his eyes to a spot before him on the floor. That was it.

I went back to my parents' home in Atlanta and worked for a year as a construction worker, trying all the while to understand what that meant. "Sit," the abbot had said. I did that every morning and every evening. The first few weeks I often cried from the pain of sitting motionless on the floor, or from the strain of trying to wrap my mind around that single word.

Eventually I returned to the monastery for further instruction (again, it wasn't much), and the following year I returned to school in Tennessee. My friends were curious about what I had been doing, and so I explained as best I could.

One night my friend Michael approached me in the dining hall carrying a large package. I was waiting in line. "This is for you," he said and thrust the package into my hands. I unwrapped the brown paper while several people looked on, and there emerged a plump black meditation cushion exactly like the ones they used in the monastery. "I made it myself," he declared, and before I could say anything he turned and disappeared into the crowd.

I don't know what struck me more, the abruptness of the gift or the fact that Michael had sewn it himself. I didn't know whether any of my friends could sew. I couldn't, and I would have been willing to bet that Michael couldn't either. But when I examined the cushion, with its elaborate pleated sides, the job was well done. I later learned that Michael could make virtually anything from a set of instructions found in a book—including tofu. In fact, he had taught himself to meditate that way.

That night I went back to my room and used the cushion for the first time. Everything was different. It wasn't the fact of the cushion per se—which I could have purchased from the monastery—but the fact that Michael had made it for me. It completely changed the way I thought of him, and the way I thought of myself.

After that night the two of us stood in relationship to something else. Suddenly what I was doing seemed less foreign—less like something I had studied at a monastery in upstate New York, and more like something I could practice where I lived.

In the years since then I have often thought about our Sewanee Zendo. Steve and Lucy got married. Michael lives in Berkeley. And all of us have gone on to do something further with Zen. But when we see one another even now, there is something more than nostalgia. And I sometimes make a kind of joke about International Dai Bosatsu Zendo, the monastery in the Catskills where I later trained and lived, because after all, a spiritual practice doesn't happen internationally. It happens where you live.

Part 2

The

Haiku

Mind

Seeds from a Birch Tree

A haiku ought to make sense literally. It must be understandable right away. The objective image is the flesh and bone of haiku. Without it there is no poem.

Here is a haiku by Sister Benedicta, an Episcopal nun whom I came to know by chance when my wife noticed her reading a book of haiku on a New York City bus.

inside our chapel

with beings of wood and stone

seeds from a birch tree

The scene is simple: through the door of the
chapel the seeds of a birch tree have blown, scat-
tering across the floor. Above and all around them
are the holy figures of a convent chapel, a place
of prayer and contemplation.

The truth of the literal, and its wordless
message, is the meaning of the poem. In Christian
terms, we might call it incarnation. I do not know
whether this understanding is in line with current
Episcopal theology, but monastics throughout the
world will understand what it means. Likewise,
anyone who follows the Way of Haiku long
enough will come to appreciate this matter. In
Buddhist terms we sometimes express the truth of
the literal with expressions such as "This very
body is the body of the Buddha," or by saying,
"All beings have the Buddha nature." Sometimes
we simply say, "samsara (the world of suffering)
is nirvana."

When I had known my second teacher, a Japanese Zen master, for some years, the time came for him to give me a Buddhist name. When the moment came, however, he only laughed and said "Kuraku," which was what he always called me anyway, being Japanese and unable to pronounce my name in English. In a strange sort of way it seemed appropriate that my name had not changed, and so I nodded, feeling pleased. But when he continued to laugh, I wasn't sure. "You see," he said, "it really *is* the perfect name for you." Until that moment it hadn't occurred to me to ask what, if anything, it meant in Japanese. When I asked, he replied, "suffering and joy."

Later that year, when I went to live in the monastery, I found the name less fortuitous than before. At odd moments during the day, always in the presence of others, my teacher would shout "Kuraku!" and then ask, "Which are you now, Ku or Raku?" And I would answer one or the other, or both, or neither, and each time he and all the others would laugh. There were times when I simply went back to my room and cried.

This sort of hazing continued for only a short time, but the matter came up again. One day after I had been living at the monastery for awhile, my teacher said that he thought he must have translated the name wrong after all. Actually, it meant "samsara and nirvana." Still later he retranslated it to mean "sometimes samsara, sometimes nirvana." Then, finally, some years later, as we were having tea, he said, "You know by now, of course, that your name means only this: samsara *is* nirvana."

Like the name Kuraku, there are many ways of expressing the truth of incarnation, but in haiku we always say it in the ordinary way. Something like "seeds from a birch tree." They also are beings. Their lightness and beauty fill the poem. And yet, the real beauty—and the thing that makes it haiku—is that the seeds remain merely seeds. They are not symbols, or a metaphor for something else. We may say "incarnation," but really that is only birch seeds. They are beings too. Artists, poets, monks, and nuns—anyone who spends a lot of time in contemplation—will understand this point. It is nothing esoteric—the seeds are not something else. Just as they are, they are holy.

Coolness

summer afternoon
the coolness of the newspaper
from the grocery bag

—Cor van den Heuvel

A refreshing moment. Plain—and very simple. But what exactly does it *mean*? Even after
having written haiku for ten or twenty years we

may sometimes ask ourselves this question. The desire for explanation is very strong.

Certain poems require no explanation. They stand for what they are. On a summer afternoon the newspaper taken out of a grocery bag feels cool. If that is not meaningful, then much of life must not be meaningful as well. The task of the haiku poet is not to explain such moments, but to live them, and to capture their life in words.

Oars

Oars flash in the sun:
at the center of the lake
Two men cease to row

—Ken Stec

This poem is a perfect example of objective description. There is nothing in the way. Oars flash. Two men stop rowing at the center of a lake. I find myself only wanting to look, not needing to say more.

Cockscombs

Masaoka Shiki is sometimes referred to as the father of modern haiku, but the truth is, his life barely poked through the bottom of this century. He died after a long bout with spinal tuberculosis in 1902, having just reached the age of thirty-five. Nevertheless, his influence on the development of modern haiku was profound. Without the freshness and vitality of Shiki's "sketch from life" doctrine, haiku might not have survived into the twentieth century, and it is doubtful whether it would have traveled from Japan to so many different countries around the world.

For almost ten years a blue slip of paper marked one poem in my book about Shiki. Although the poem was composed in the classical five-seven-five syllable form, because of its utter simplicity, it seems best to report it literally, along with Shiki's headnote:

Before the Garden

cockscombs . . .
must be 14,
or 15

—Masaoka Shiki
(trans. by
Janine Beichman)

I loved this haiku from the very first time I read it. Although I had never seen cockscombs, I had some vague notion of what they looked like merely from the name: bright red flowers resembling a rooster's comb.

I left the slip of paper there because the poem remained a puzzle. However much I loved it, I would never have quoted it as an example of haiku for fear of being ridiculed. I simply couldn't justify my fondness for it at all, even after having read the various commentaries by Japanese critics who contrasted, for instance, Shiki the invalid and the vertical stalks of fiery red autumn flowers in his little garden—the garden which, other than the faces of those who came to visit, was the only thing he had to look at during the last six years of his life. Or the feeling—thought by some to be implicit to the poem—that the flowers would survive him into autumn. Privately, however, Shiki's cockscombs set a kind of personal standard by which I judged every poem I wrote. I felt certain they had something to do with the Haiku Mind, but I had no idea what that something might be.

Nearly a decade passed. My first marriage had ended in divorce, and after a time spent in the monastery, I left the monkhood and returned to haiku and the life of a layman, where I first began. Finally, I remarried. My wife and I had just moved into a new apartment in Manhattan with a garden in the back. The garden was a real treasure. The floor was red brick, with a narrow raised border for flowers running along three sides. In back of it was, not another building, but the playground of a public elementary school. We planted daffodils and crocuses, jewelweed and dusty miller. We bought a bird feeder, and soon the garden was filled every day with sparrows.

One day that first autumn my wife came home from the Korean market with a large bunch of very unusual flowers—if you could call them that. They looked more like bunches of stiff red velvet folded over many times and affixed to the tops of greenish-purple rods. When I tried to arrange them, the stalks were difficult to separate. I had to bear down hard with the knife, using both hands on the blade, to cut through them.

"What *are* these?" I asked.

"Cockscombs," she replied.

I was astonished. In that moment I realized that I had missed everything about the poem. I hadn't understood Shiki's flowers at all. Not their weight or texture. Not their color, or the firmness of their stalks. Nor the way they clustered together, making a precise count of them difficult from whatever angle, and impossible from any distance at all. I think it was then that I began to realize that Shiki's counting had been entirely without design. In his mind there had been no impulse to acquire or to assign any value over what was there before the eye. And once I understood this, I found that for the first time I also understood the photograph of Shiki which had hung above my desk for many years.

In the photo, Shiki is propped up on one hand looking out from the verandah of his house. This is the meaning of the headnote, "Before the Garden": Shiki lying just like this, leaning up on one hand looking out. The time seems to be dusk, or perhaps a very cloudy day, for the face is luminous. Over one shoulder a shutter looms white at the end of the room behind him.

It is the eyes which always stir me most: clear, calm, perhaps a little detached. Their vision is plain, even literal. It is a gaze in which intelligence, not yet having come to rest on any single thought, is everywhere apparent in the air about the body, which is also like an eye. Dark as it is, the photograph shimmers with its light.

What I had missed about the cockscombs all those years was the feeling of their reality, of their being fully present in the world. And connected, to every other life, by the season and the feeling of a single moment happening now.

I knew then for the first time that the true significance of Shiki's cockscombs lay in the flowers themselves, and not in some other, metaphorical meaning, however apt or true. It may take a lifetime to come to an understanding which is clear, direct, and very simple. But the primary work of haiku is always a restoration of the world.

The famous modern critic Kenkichi Yamamoto once wrote:

> Every masterpiece is a flower on a precipice ... It is a tremendous assertion for the poet to have said, "There must be fourteen or fifteen stalks of cockscomb." After we read this poem we cannot imagine the possibility that there could have been more or fewer cockscombs than fourteen or fifteen.

For some time I was very impressed with this statement, but it now seems to me that the American scholar Donald Keene may have come closer to the truth of Shiki's poem when he wrote, "Probably Shiki composed the haiku easily, even artlessly, as he looked at the garden, unaware that he had created a masterpiece of haiku ..."

All that was required of the moment spent looking at cockscombs was a simple, artless exclamation on their number. The failure to assign one value over another gives the haiku a spiritual clarity and justice that transcends a mere accounting of the world. Moreover, the statement of a second number does not indicate indecision, but an extension and intensification of simple wonder by the interval of one stalk.

The real power of the poem, then, lies not in the fact that it is a "tremendous assertion," as Yamamoto has said, but that it is a very small one. In it there is no violence to the spirit or to the world. Ultimately, the number of flowers cannot be precisely reckoned. And it is this slight element of uncertainty—of humility, or simply play—which brings the moment to its peak and, with the smallest adjustment, aligns the human heart in friendship with autumn flowers and all the many beings of this world.

Daisies

Those who have done the meditation practice of following the breath know something about haiku. If you sit in a relaxed, upright position and watch closely as each breath comes in and goes out of the body, you will notice that, although the mind is sometimes dull and fuzzy, there comes a moment every now and then when it is not distracted, when it is not doing anything but following the breath. In such moments it may seem as though nothing could possibly be so clear.

Almost at once, however, we seize upon this clear breath as the object of our meditation practice—as the goal we have been trying to achieve. Immediately the mind stumbles and ceases to flow. The problem is this: rather than just looking at the breath, we want to watch ourselves looking at it. We want to include the self. We want some judgment.

Gradually, however, we learn just to look at the breath without becoming too invested in whether we are really looking or not—without trying to determine whether or not the meditation is working and we are making progress. This is real looking.

When we speak about oneness in meditation or in haiku, we tend to get locked into a fixed idea. That idea then becomes a block to understanding what oneness really is.

Oneness is there already when we look at nature. A daisy, for instance. We look at its whiteness, its yellow face, the green stem coming up to the ankle or the calves. Merely looking at a daisy we achieve oneness on the spot. No need even to say "achieve." Oneness is there already. Looking itself is oneness. Looking is the *activity* of oneness.

A problem comes up, however, when we say to ourselves, "I am looking at a daisy." When we do that, then it seems, in fact, there must be some separation. "I am here, and the daisy is there, and I am looking at it." When we say it that way, the oneness is lost. If we don't say it, but continue looking, there is the realization of oneness with a daisy. Then everything is perfectly precise and clear.

I learned to look at daisies from Nakagawa Soen Roshi, a Japanese Zen master whom I met briefly in 1982.

I had been practicing Zen for a few years when I finally summoned up the courage to attend my first week-long silent retreat at Dai Bosatsu Zendo, the monastery in the Catskills. I was nervous and afraid, but determined to get through it if I possibly could. As an added incentive, I was told that Soen Roshi would be in attendance for the first time in several years. I had by that time heard many stories about his eccentric style of teaching and had learned, in particular, that he had written haiku all his life and that many were considered to be fine Zen poems. Like his friend Nyogen Senzaki, he sometimes even used haiku as a way of teaching Zen. So it seemed as though I might possibly get the opportunity to ask his understanding of the Zen of haiku.

It was a huge retreat. People had come from all over the world to attend it. Soen Roshi gave a talk every day, and the fourth day, according to tradition, was available for private interviews. When that day arrived, the students were called row by row from the meditation hall. Every few minutes a bell would sound, indicating that an interview was over, and a monk would strike another bell in the room where students waited in silence. Then the next person would rise and proceed down a long polished corridor to the small room where Soen Roshi waited quietly, seated in meditation.

I was at the end of the last row, the least senior of all the students. When my turn finally came, I positioned myself on the cushion in front of the bell as the others had done. But when Soen Roshi rang his bell, the monk struck twice in answer, signaling the end of the session. I was told to return to the meditation hall. The time allotted for the interviews was at an end, and I would not be able to speak with him alone.

A few days later the retreat was over. My teacher assured me that I had done very well, but the truth was, I felt like a failure. I had barely made it though the week of silence and meditation. It was difficult to walk, and I had lost the feeling along the tops of both of my feet. I was sure that I could never endure such a thing again. My spiritual career was at an end.

After the retreat was over, Soen Roshi was as playful as a clown. At one point, he stripped down to his loincloth in the meal hall in order to demonstrate the pathways of the acupuncture meridians and certain pressure points that could be used to relieve pain and stiffness between periods of zazen. Later that evening he appeared at the back of the room in the guest house wearing the devil mask from a Nō drama, a chenille bedspread pulled up over his head, while he recited a speech from *Faust* as the full moon rose over the lake. The next night there was a lunar eclipse, and I have heard stories about his behavior on that night, roaming around Beecher Lake like a ghost, but I did not witness any of that. I was exhausted and slept the whole night through.

During all this time he was continually surrounded by adoring American students, for whom he was by that time already a kind of legend. Once he sat next to me on the verandah before lunch, but we did not speak. He opened his mouth wide and tilted back his head as if swallowing the sunlight and seemed almost to be asleep. I have seen dead people since that time. On one occasion, a tea master, lying on a bed. With her head tilted back on the pillow, her mouth formed the shape of a bowl. At the time it struck me she looked exactly like Soen Roshi had on the verandah. But for me, all that is beside the point.

The next day I went for a walk down the mountain toward the gate house. It was then that I met Soen Roshi alone. He also was just out walking. As we neared each other, I summoned up my courage and introduced myself. I told him that I had hoped to meet him during the retreat, but that it turned out that was not possible. He offered me his hand and we shook. Then, suddenly, I didn't have anything to say. I couldn't bear to ask him about haiku. It just didn't seem to matter. It seemed to me that this was the only encounter I would ever have with this man, and I was filled with sadness. I liked him very much.

For some reason he made no move to depart and walk on despite my inability to speak. Finally, he bent over and pointed at a flower growing by the road. "What do you call this?" he asked.

I couldn't speak at all. I had read Zen books on similar dialogues for years and could not begin to fathom them. It seemed the more of them I read the less I understood. I wasn't even sure I had understood a single thing from any of his talks during the retreat. I suddenly felt as though I wanted to cry. But then he smiled and said, "No. Just its name. What is its name?"

I was so relieved. "Daisy," I answered. "It is called a daisy."

"Daisy," he repeated, bending down close and drawing out the word as though he were tasting its flavor. "Beautiful flower! Beautiful!" And he continued on his way, while I looked after him, his small back bending slightly this way and that as he climbed the hill.

I do not remember when it first occurred to me that I had missed something in this encounter, but it must have been about the time of Soen's death in 1984. Still, it was only a decade after that that I understood what he had meant.

According to Takahama Kyoshi, the proper subject of haiku is to sing the beauty of birds and flowers. However, few people in this life encounter circumstances which allow them to realize this flower mind. So haiku is a gentle discipline to help the world along the road to its realization. It does not matter if it is sometimes regarded as a second-class art. It does not matter if that mind sees buildings, cooling-towers, or a rose. What matters is that we realize it clearly while we are alive. When asked what his best haiku was, Soen Roshi always replied,

Hana no yo no
Hana no yoh naru
Hito bakari

The meaning is in the sound and rhythm and the way the three parts make a whole, but it translates roughly, "All beings are blossoms blossoming in a blossoming universe"—a scene of cherry blossoms on a hillside, or maybe in a park. If one truly understands a poem like this, it is unnecessary to study haiku.

Haiku Mind

When you count the syllables for a haiku on your fingers and select a season word, already you have touched the mind of Bashō and all the other haiku poets of the past. How could it be otherwise than this? People ask me what Haiku Mind is, and I offer various explanations in accordance with the place and time, but the truth is, it is only this.

A haiku is a seventeen-syllable poem on a subject drawn from nature. This is both the simplest explanation and the secret of the art. In reality, however, this explanation is no different than what can be found in any good dictionary of American English. It reflects no hidden teaching. "A seventeen-syllable verse form divided into lines of five-seven-five and having a reference to nature or the season" is an explanation so simple and straightforward that anyone—even a child—can understand and practice it right away.

I stress its importance again, not because it is difficult to grasp, but because it expresses the proper frame of mind for composing haiku, which is the one thing everyone forgets. Somehow it tends to become overcomplicated or obscured over the course of study. Or we develop the idea that we should go beyond it—beyond what is simple and plain. Therefore, it needs to be reclarified at every stage of practice before going on. A haiku is a seventeen-syllable poem.

In July 1993, the poet Katō Shuson passed away at the age of eighty-eight. One of the greatest haiku poets of this century, for many years he selected poems for the weekly haiku column of the *Asahi Shimbun,* one of Japan's largest newspapers.

According to a newspaper story written by

English haiku poet James Kirkup, two weeks before he died, Shuson fell into a coma and never regained consciousness. Even while he lay unconscious, however, his fingers continued to move in the syllable-counting fashion typical of Japanese haiku poets: "bending the fingers inward toward the palm, then releasing them again one by one."

Sound

Whether written in English or Japanese, a haiku is poetry, not prose. That is, its purpose is not to convey information, but the feeling of a particular place and time. And in haiku, as in all forms of poetry, feeling lies in sound.

Every phenomenon in the universe—even silence—has a certain sound. If we hum a light-hearted tune for a while, we will find that its effect on our state of mind is different than if we hummed a somber one. Likewise, it is better to grunt than whistle when lifting something heavy. Just so with poetry.

The art of haiku lies in finding a rhythm and tonal quality which fall precisely in a slot with the feeling of a particular moment in place and time. When this has been accomplished, we find a seamless quality to the language of the poem. It is almost as though it had disappeared— it is there, and yet it is not.

We can analyze the poem to see why it works, but our first impression is simply that it does—that it sounds like what it says.

the cardinal's call
drills a row of scarlet holes
in the summer air

—Alfred Marks

in the windless heat
the custodian's dustmop
propped against the gate

—Jerry Ball

lifting the seaweed
clusters of periwinkles
attached to the rocks

—Susan Rudnick

before the rainstorm
warm breezes turn leaves over
to the silver side

          —Jody Kimmel

autumn butterfly—
flutters in an empty jar
of blueberry jam

          —Dennis Davidson

The
Elastic
Moment

Beginners often develop the misconception that haiku come like a flash of lightning, but this is very seldom so. Even when a poem comes out finished on the spot, the process isn't so tight as that. We must allow a little space within which to compose the poem. The longer we practice haiku, the more we will come to understand that there is no need to be frantic or hurried. There is always plenty of time.

When I first began to serve as an officer in

the monastery, I sometimes felt overwhelmed at
the number of things that needed to be taken care
of. Given the rigors of the training schedule, when
other duties were added on, I often wondered how
I would get everything done.

Noticing my dilemma, a Japanese monk who
happened to be living at the monastery for a time
made a valuable suggestion. "This month you are
the Roshi's assistant," he explained. "That means
you're getting a lot of extra teaching, so keep your
eyes open."

I had been told things like this before, but
it never seemed to work. My teacher was friendly
enough, and would have answered any question I
asked him, but he was ultimately inscrutable. I
had no idea what was going on inside his mind.
I wouldn't have even known what to ask about.
So after a few days I went back to this monk and
asked what I ought to look for. He only sighed a
little and finally said, "Just watch the way he eats.
That's all. Just look at that."

But he didn't need to press the point; I knew
what he meant already. I had been sitting next to
my teacher for some time during the meals. Con-
ducted in silence according to an exacting ritual,

these meals rarely lasted more than twenty minutes. At least half of that time was devoted to chanting and serving one another, however, so there was rarely more than ten minutes left to eat. I felt resentful. As hard as I had to work, it seemed at least I ought to be allowed to finish a decent meal. And yet, while I rushed to finish eating during the allotted time, my teacher—who took the same amount of food—never seemed to hurry and always finished on time. He would take one bite and chew it slowly, sometimes even resting his chopsticks in his lap before taking another bite. There was no trick to it. He simply ate his meal in a relaxed and open way.

It took time, but I eventually discovered that if I just stopped worrying about results and kept my mind calmly focused on the task at hand, I could finish whatever I had to do. And I tended to enjoy myself more in the process.

In the beginning most of us are distrustful of inspiration. It seems to come and go in a flash without any explanation. The temptation is to grasp frantically at such moments when they occur, or to force them when they don't. Of course, neither method produces haiku.

This is where the paradox of haiku begins to emerge. For if we cultivate a strong desire to write a haiku, haiku will never come. In the absence of that desire, however, the frantic, grasping quality of mind disappears, and inspiration is free to do its work at somewhat more leisure. In Japanese, this quality of mind, at once fully engaged and detached from concern with a result, is called *furyu* (wind flow), which is a lovely way of describing how inspiration works naturally, even playfully, in accordance with circumstances as they arise.

old crabapple tree—
too early, but anyway
J give it a shake

• Try This •

Step out into your garden, or walk to a local park or forest. If you live on the ocean, walk down to the shore. Once you have arrived, confine yourself to an area immediately around you.

- Write a haiku about something you can see or hear, something you can smell or touch on that very spot. Notice the sky above you, the temperature of the air on your face. Notice especially the things on the ground right below your feet.

- When you have written one haiku, immediately write another, without pausing to consider whether it is good or bad. And when you have finished that haiku, write yet another, and then another. And so on . . .

* Continue writing haiku like this until you have twenty or thirty poems. Don't get stuck writing about the same thing if it seems too difficult. Change subjects as often as you want.

Masaoka Shiki suggested this as an exercise for writing haiku, and many Japanese poets still write haiku this way today. Shiki felt that the subjects for haiku were all around us and that if you wrote only one or two haiku at a sitting, not only would you overlook many good subjects, but your chances of getting a good haiku were fairly slim. If you wrote twenty or thirty haiku on an outing, Shiki suggested, then at least one or two of them would be good—or, at the very least, worth keeping as a record of the day.

jumping off the path
a field cricket bangs his head
on the chain-link fence

—Jeffrey Rabkin

scattered in the shrubs
unceremoniously—
the poison ivy

—Dennis Davidson

deep inside the woods
where the breeze cannot reach us
the mosquitoes bite

—Nadine Maleski

walking in dead leaves—
sending the sparrows flying
further down the path

—James Kirkup

a white tree fungus—
on the soft gray underside,
several thousand holes

—Kathy Nolan

Revision

I seldom revise the poems I compose from nature. What is important is the life of every day. I have not always subscribed to this attitude, however. It was a decision I came to after many years. What I discovered was that other people tended to prefer the haiku I dashed off on the spot; they were seldom moved by the ones I had labored over. Eventually, as I came to understand haiku more fully, I too preferred the ones that came naturally.

It may take many years of practice to find one's proper relationship to nature. During that time we are sometimes successful in writing haiku, and sometimes not. But we always learn something about what kind of effort makes good haiku. Clearly, too much effort, working and re-working, spoils a haiku. Too little effort, on the other hand, may result in a haiku that simply falls apart for lack of skill or genuine feeling. In order to find the right kind of effort, it is necessary to remain close to the source. For this reason Masaoka Shiki advocated "the sketch from nature"— composing haiku on the spot.

If we want to use haiku as a spiritual practice, the most important thing is to be fully present. My Japanese Zen teacher used to say, "No dress rehearsal!" He meant, "This is it! Now! This moment of life is unrepeatable."

People who revise their haiku endlessly tend not to have realized this unrepeatable quality of life. Because they have failed to grasp the uniqueness of each new moment, they must experiment endlessly after the fact in the hope of finding it. And because this process tends to involve so much self-conscious effort, it often results in a feeling of attachment to the poem. It has strings attached—subtle expectations by the poet which the reader can sense behind the words—the expectation for instance that the reader will get a certain humor or meaning from the poem. But these things are no substitute for the feeling of reality we find in a haiku written directly from life.

I said originally that poets who revise too much have not yet realized the unrepeatable quality of life, but they also suffer a deficiency in the quality of their relationship to the world, for that relationship loses its flexibility and vigor in the course of reworking a poem. Moreover, composing a haiku by revision is unlikely to result in the kind of clarity, the feeling of reality that is the unique hallmark of haiku and the true source of its meaning.

Directness

Someone once said to me that he thought the style of e e. cummings' shorter poems was more direct than haiku. I replied that, although I enjoyed those poems, it was difficult to say them aloud in the ordinary way and that, consequently, they were less direct than haiku, which are always straightforward and plain.

"Well, what about William Carlos Williams then?" he asked, suggesting the following well-known poem:

so much depends

upon

a red wheel

barrow

glazed with rain

water

beside the white

chickens

"Better," I replied. "But we still notice the form too much."

Moreover, there is a certain self-consciousness to the placement of the words upon the page. Unsurprisingly, the poet also feels the need to tell us how to respond to the image. Williams didn't do this in all of his poems—often he let the image speak for itself. But on this occasion, perhaps because he wasn't yet used to working in a very short form, he felt the need to say "so much depends upon."

A haiku poet has already accepted the significance of ordinary events in daily life. Haiku was born of a tradition that celebrates the very "ordinariness" of life. As haiku poets, we also accept seventeen syllables as the given form. As this acceptance deepens over time, our poetry becomes paradoxically more artless and more profound. Artless because, by perfecting the form, we forget the form. Profound because, when this artless expression finally comes, our poetry begins to flow directly out of life.

It is a misunderstanding to suppose that directness is an artistic technique that one can master. Directness come from life.

Restraint

As modern human beings we spend much
of our lives wrapped up inside ourselves. The
Way of Haiku is to "come unwrapped" and
thereby notice what lies outside of the self.
Without unwrapping ourselves, it is not possible
to follow nature; it is not even possible to notice nature, much less to look carefully and with
heart.

Too often we become more interested in being artful than in depicting a scene from nature.

When this happens, whether we realize it or not, our focus has shifted from nature to the self.

The scholar R. H. Blyth explained that a haiku is a finger pointing at the moon. If the finger itself is too beautiful, then we will notice the finger, not the moon. Likewise, of course, it must not be ugly. In that case also we would notice the finger instead.

The object of haiku is always to point at the moon. Therefore, a haiku must be neither too polished, nor very coarse. In either case, the poem would become an end in itself, rather than a way to look at nature. This is the reason why the best haiku often look so plain.

There is one thing in particular that we can practice in writing haiku that will help us to "unwrap" ourselves, and that is restraint. In haiku there is a kind of unwritten rule prohibiting overt displays of emotion or intellect. Putting too much of our own emotion in a haiku tends to displace what Bashō called "the feelings emanating from the thing itself." Likewise with intellection: if we assign some special meaning to a scene from nature, then we have merely projected our thoughts upon it. These thoughts become like a film of dust covering a pair of eyeglasses—only when we clean the lenses do we realize how dirty they had become.

a yellow sunset:
it's cool outside the restaurant
after eating fish

Crab

In time of danger
the crab only needs to go
into a drainpipe.

—Yamaguchi Seishi
(trans. by Alfred Marks
and Takashi Kodaira)

About this poem the poet wrote only:

When danger approaches a crab, he runs
and hides, like the crab I watched flee to
safety in a drainpipe. A crab finds it simple
to save his life.

The poet makes no mention of the house he
lost in a bombing raid only a few years before,
but the feeling of that loss—and other, more sig-
nificant losses from World War II—permeates the
poem.

Diver

Diver in the air
how little time goes by before
he hits the water!

       —Yamaguchi Seishi

       (trans. by Alfred Marks

       and Takashi Kodaira)

Seishi's comment:

A diver stands on a diving platform, then he pushes off the platform and dives into the pool. The time between the platform and the pool is very short—the time it takes a man to fall.

A reflection on the brevity of life—so simple, so perfect, it would have been a shame to say anything more.

Ears

Sentimentality ruins haiku. The same can be said of most other kinds of poetry. When we exaggerate our emotion, it becomes a burden to the reader, making it difficult to experience the poem. What, then, is sentimentality, and how do we avoid it?

Sentimentality is self-conscious emotion. It happens when, in the midst of an emotion, we want to watch ourselves *having* that emotion. In such moments, the feeling turns too sweet. It becomes self-consciously precious or sad—in other words, something other than it is, if only in degree.

The way to avoid sentimentality is simple. In the midst of an emotion, we stay with the image itself. If we can train ourselves to do this, the result will be a deeper, truer kind of poem. Consider the following haiku:

East winds blow—

ears emerge from

nape-length hair

—Sugita Hisajo

(trans. by Janine Beichman)

Hisajo was a student of Takahama Kyoshi. In this poem, a young girl (perhaps her daughter) is standing outside, or maybe walking on her way to school. Her hair has the bob-cut traditional for Japanese schoolgirls. Its rich blackness completely frames her face. Until the warm east winds blow. When that happens, the wind parts the hair at the sides, and ears emerge. Hisajo has caught the moment before sweetness goes too far. The result is a moment of oneness with the wind.

Two
Stones

One day an American woman who had been studying gardening for some time in Japan went to see her teacher. When they had greeted one another, he said, "Today I have to decide about two stones." Then, taking a large piece of chalk from the shelf, on the surface of the workbench he traced the path along which they were to be placed. "What do you think?" he asked, and handed her two stones of uneven size.

Examining them, the woman noticed that

they fit nicely together along the left of the path. "No. That's all wrong," the teacher said. "You've made them look the same." "Okay," she replied, "then what about this?" and she placed the stones about a foot apart, so that, having taken a turn in the path just beyond the first gray boulder, the second would become visible in just that moment. "Very sad," was her teacher's reply. "Now the stones can no longer see one another—if the smaller one sighs, the larger one will never hear." After that the student tried several other configurations, taking longer to consider between each one. But her teacher only leaned against the door-jamb and shook his head. Finally, he stepped outside to resume some other project, leaving the woman alone.

The student was in despair. "I'll never learn," she told herself. "Maybe I ought to go back to America, because if I'm really honest I have to admit that I have no understanding even after all these years. My teacher is just too kind to tell me I've been wasting his time." And with this last thought she turned to leave the shed. As she was walking out, however, she realized that she was still holding the stones, one in each hand, so she placed them on the bench and left.

She had walked all the way back out to the road when she remembered herself. "It would be rude to leave without saying goodbye. He will only worry if I don't return." So she retraced her steps to the little shed. When she entered, however, her teacher barely greeted her. Instead, he remained facing the stones as she had left them. After a while he said, "Yes. We will place the stones this way."

Bashō once said that a haiku is made by combining things. In practice, this means that a haiku is usually composed of two parts: a five-syllable phrase followed by a twelve-syllable one, or just the reverse. One phrase sets forth the season, the other juxtaposes some other image. This arrangement of images in a formal pattern is governed by a principle which the Japanese call *niku issho:* "two phrases, one poem." In other words, though the two parts remain distinct, together they form an impression which is more than the sum of their parts—that is, together they form a poem.

Needless to say, it can be difficult to place two images together in a sincere, original way; otherwise, haiku poets would not have labored for so many centuries over the art of juxtaposition. Strictly speaking, the work is never done. The pairing of images must be mastered every time we write a poem.

late winter snowstorm:
a button pops off & clicks
on the wooden floor

Breaking

the

Form

Knowing where and when to break the traditional form, and how much to break it, is a mark
of mastery in the art of haiku. Because the form
itself is the rule, there can be no established rule
on how to break it. Only about 4 percent of classical haiku depart from the five-seven-five form,
and even then, usually by not more than one syllable. And there are other, less obvious aspects of
the genre which can sometimes be tested while
keeping within the spirit of haiku—the limita-

tion, for instance, to one event happening now.

Suffice it to say, if a poet never breaks the form, that poet may not be really alive within it; whereas the poet who breaks it all the time isn't really writing haiku.

In the early decades of this century there was a movement away from the traditional form of Japanese haiku. Called the New Trend School, these poets—some of whom also later rejected the use of season words—wrote poems of more, or even less, than the traditional seventeen syllables. The movement included many fine poets, such as Kawahigashi Hekigoto and Ogiwara Seisensui. The New Trend movement soon fell away from the mainstream, however, and the classical norm returned.

It seems to me that the proper understanding of free-meter haiku is that the traditional form, so firmly established over the centuries, actually permitted such a departure. In other words, people tended to hear the traditional form *within* poems that were longer, or superimposed over those which fell short of the traditional length. Paradoxically, then, the form continued to work to the advantage of those very poets who violated it. With time, however, that form was lost for the lack of clear defining limits. The dissatisfaction that grew out of this loss was evidently so profound by 1929 that Takahama Kyoshi, the editor of the magazine *Hototogisu* (Cuckoo), had only to announce that, in his opinion, haiku was a classical literary form written in the traditional way, and the demise of the New Trend Haiku was virtually assured.

So the form itself establishes the limits to which it can be taken. Earlier I said that there was no rule about breaking the form. But that is not entirely true. If breaking the form in a particular instance preserves the spirit of haiku, then the poet must break the form. Indeed, in such a case, abiding by the form would have killed that spirit. Even so, this is seldom really necessary to do.

long winter night
J open the red cookie tin
for needle and thread

—Carl Patrick

summer evening—
a park ranger's brief lecture
about wildflowers

—Jerry Ball

on the Chinese vase
flowers retain brightness—
pouring out water

—Dave McCroskey

green awning—
a waterpail left in the doorway
catches summer light

        —Christine Shook

a cool August day—
the nylon quilt I washed
has lost its flowers

        —Sister Benedicta

Zen
Tea

Once when I was visiting one of my Zen friends, he offered to make me some tea. When he went into the kitchen, however, he discovered he was out of tea bags. So he brought two cups in anyway. Placing one of them before me, he said simply, "Zen tea." And we both laughed.

Probably, you have heard this kind of joke before. It plays upon the popular understanding of Zen as something empty. My friend was making fun of that idea. He was actually sorry that he had no tea to offer, so he offered the joke instead.

The sort of empty-headed Zen my friend was making fun of actually gets a lot of play in American haiku. A well-known poet once printed a single word in the middle of a page and called it haiku. The poem caused a lot of discussion among American haiku poets. Some said it was a haiku, others said not. The real surprise was that there was any discussion in the first place. It should have been obvious to anyone who understood haiku that, if anything, it was only a kind of joke.

The point is this: the first time you are served Zen tea it is delightful; thereafter, it is only a disappointment.

Haiku
and
Zen
Poetry

In general, it is permissible to say that haiku is a type of Zen poetry, but in light of recent poems published under that guise, we might better say that it is not. Not Zen poetry the way it has come to be known in America today. In fact, haiku is different even from the traditional Zen poetry of China and Japan.

In practice, Zen poetry alludes to or takes as its subject some aspect of the doctrine, history, or practice of Zen. Its purpose is nearly always to convey some sense of the fundamental truth of Buddhist teaching. In the history of Zen (both in Japan and in China, where Zen was known as *Ch'an*), there have been many fine examples of this kind of poem. Today, many readers are familiar with names like Po Chu-i, Ikkyu, and Ryokan.

Even in America there are a few poems to be found, for instance among those of W. S. Merwin, which convey the truth of Zen. In most of what has been offered by Americans as Zen poetry, however, there is a layer of spiritual posturing which—once you know what to look for—is as easy to tell from the real thing as night from day.

In haiku there must be no posturing at all—especially *spiritual* posturing. I often say to students that when they have composed a real haiku, that is the point at which we can legitimately begin to talk about their verse in terms of Zen. A Zen haiku is simply an ordinary haiku composed in the ordinary way. I have noticed, however, that almost no one is able to do this. The object is not to create some special kind of poem, but merely to relax into the moment as it is and abide there peacefully, even in the act of composing a poem. Almost always there is some subtle posturing.

Though students who come to my workshops are often surprised when I present the basic principles of haiku, and want to write some seemingly freer or more difficult kind of poem, I always ask them just to try it anyway. It seems that very quickly they realize its challenges, and by the end of the workshop everyone has some understanding of how haiku can be used as a spiritual practice. And those who have come expecting to write a Zen poem discover firsthand that this cannot be accomplished merely by a wink at the Buddha, but must arise directly from the Haiku Mind.

Part 3

The

Narrow

Road

The Way North

Haiku, in many ways the most outward, most concrete, and most perceptually grounded form of poetry, is also the most inward. It requires a lot of inner work. Bashō titled his greatest work *Oku no Hosomichi (The Narrow Road to the Deep North)*. Bashō traveled a long way north on a journey with his student and fellow poet Sora and kept a diary of his travels. The diary contains many of his most famous haiku.

So *The Narrow Road to the Deep North* is

a tangible, outward journey. That is one way of looking at it. But *oku* also means "within," so you could say one or the other—"the way north" or "the way within"—and both are true, and neither is. Bashō's understanding, and the reason I think he chose a title that suggests both meanings, is that the way north *is* the way within. This kind of understanding comes when we realize that in looking out, we are also looking in. We learn it by looking very carefully at the world.

Haiku is both a very outward and a profoundly contemplative, inner kind of art. It is not possible to sacrifice either *way* and still be writing haiku. If we only understand looking out, our poems will have no heart. If only looking in, they are likely to become self-indulgent or obscure. So both are necessary. Shiki came to understand these two aspects of haiku in terms of *makoto*, sincere feeling, and *shasei*, the sketch from nature. But really, they are not two separate things.

A Baby's Head

turnip in my hand—
its cold roundness heavier
than a baby's head

—Sister Benedicta

This poem won first prize in a contest which was judged by a Japanese haiku master. In his commentary on the poem, the judge wrote, "At some time in her life the poet must have cradled a dead baby in her arms."

Sister Benedicta was surprised when she read this comment. She told me that she had simply taken a turnip from the refrigerator when, holding in her hand, the image of a baby's head came to mind. In fact, she had never held a dead baby. But when I reminded her of the events of sixty years ago, her eyes filled up with tears.

Sister Benedicta was born in Spain just prior to the Spanish Civil War. When the war began her father, the novelist Ramón José Sender, escaped on foot over the mountains, thinking that the authorities would not harm his wife and child. However, not long thereafter, mother and baby were imprisoned. One day a few months later, her mother was taken out to the graveyard and shot. The man who carried out the execution was a local official whose advances she had spurned several years before.

Some of you may have heard the story of her daughter Andrea Sender, who refused to eat and eventually died in prison after her mother was shot. Mistakenly reported in newspapers all over the world, the story of Sister Benedicta's death persists to the present day.

Easter
Lilies

the Easter lilies:
no matter how you turn them
blossoms face the wall

—Sister Benedicta

Easter lilies grow in such a way that the large white blossoms face opposite directions on the stalk. Perhaps it is natural to want them all to face the front, so that their beauty can be appreciated. But that is not possible. Whichever way you turn them, some blossoms face the wall.

Bugs

whatever has cut
the round holes in these round leaves
has carried them off

—Sister Benedicta

A haiku almost never fails to state clearly
what is being described or talked about. But this
poem breaks that rule in a playful manner. The
time is probably late summer, when the leaves

are ripe for the harvest of the bugs. At the moment of composition, however, they have already gone, carrying the holes off with them.

The poet's observation is tinged with melancholy, but there is a kind of deadpan quality to the observation that also makes it funny, and then there's the idea of the empty spaces—the holes themselves—being carried off. Is that even possible? It seems to tease the mind.

Leaf
Stem

The place where the leaf
has left the stem is perfect
for just that purpose

—Sister Benedicta

The time is autumn, and the poet has noticed the place where a leaf has left the stem.
Looking closely, she sees a notch. Perfect.

As human beings we tend to live in fear of

death. Perhaps this is natural. And yet, it must be just as natural to die. In the history of the world, there is no one who has not died. Throughout our lives, on some level or another, we struggle with the idea of death. But the moment of our departure has been provided for.

Openness

I often say that haiku come out of the place where objective description overlaps the heart. In other words, where the image itself expresses precisely how we feel. At such moments we do not know whether nature came first, and then the feeling, or whether the feeling was there already and simply found its proper expression in a scene from nature. In either case, it is important to realize that this can only happen when we make space enough in the heart for nature to overlap it, and space enough in nature for the play and exercise of the heart.

It is essential to understand that the art of haiku is both passive and active. I have sometimes heard the expression "meditation in action." Haiku is exactly that. Indeed, each of the Zen arts could be said to be a way of cultivating active meditation, meditative action.

Snow

One day I was out walking in the mountains. When I left home the weather had been clear, but soon it began to snow. I might have turned back, but I was in an expansive mood. As I now recall it, the feeling I had on that day was quite extraordinary. It was as if my Zen training and all the other things I had done with my life had come full circle and merged with haiku. I felt wondrously alone and sublime.

At one point I realized that if I climbed a little higher I would come to a large basin in the mountain which ought to be quite scenic with all the freshly fallen snow. In fact, on the way up I was so overcome with the anticipation of its beauty that I composed a Zen poem:

after a long climb
only my feet have printed
the basin of snow

As I continued to climb, I repeated the verse many times to taste its sound, and the more I repeated it the more perfectly it seemed to reflect the condition of having attained the Haiku Mind. Of course, other people had attained it before me— there were Bashō and Shiki at least. But that experience, I told myself, was always a kind of fundamental aloneness. Likewise, the more I thought about the image of a basin full of snow open to the high mountain sky, the more perfect a representation it seemed of the Haiku Mind. And of course, there was the "long climb"—I had been practicing many years by then. And so with all of these thoughts in mind, I reached the lip of the basin.

It was more beautiful even than I had imagined. I stood there a moment just to take it in before walking down a ways. But before I had taken three steps I began to slide. Underneath the freshly fallen snow, there were inches of perfectly slick ice. Before I knew it my feet had gone from underneath me and I had slid halfway down the basin. My cotton pants and canvas jacket were covered in snow and my hands were frozen. The only thing that stopped my descent was this one small tree to which I clung desperately, unable even to stand, much less climb back up to the rim. It continued to snow and now I really *was* alone. I realized that no one would pass this way today, nor perhaps tomorrow. I looked back up at the basin rim, and there indeed were my footprints—the only pair.

I lay there getting colder and colder, finally clinging with my arms because my hands would no longer hold. I suppose the only thing I can say for myself is that in former years I would have clung there to that tree even longer than I did. But eventually I did the only sensible thing and let go, sliding to the very bottom of the bowl where I could stand. From there actually I realized it wasn't a basin at all. There was a slight declivity leading down out of the far side. So I was able to stand up and simply walk right out.

My hands wouldn't work properly for a while, but otherwise I was none the worse for wear. I had to laugh at myself, though. I had been in trouble with snow before. A number of years earlier I had gone for a walk with my friend Seiko. We left the monastery one morning after the conclusion of a week-long silent retreat, having packed a bag lunch for the day. We intended to find the cave where Soen Roshi was supposed to have meditated when living there one winter years before. We found what we thought was the cave because it had a cairn of stones before it, and after lunch came right back down the mountain because it had begun to snow—a late spring blizzard.

Only, somehow, we came down the wrong

side of a ridge and ended up walking far into a trailless area of the Catskill Mountain State Preserve. The snow was blinding, and we were underdressed and ill-equipped. We hadn't a single match between us. We wandered lost for many hours, climbing to the tops of ridges when the sky briefly cleared, only to find the mountains all looked the same. And wherever we walked the snow erased our steps.

Finally, completely exhausted, we just sat down, unable to move. At that moment, however, I noticed a walking stick leaning up against a tree and, in an act of faith, because I did not know what else to do, I simply picked it up and began to walk in that direction, chanting a short sutra because I had no energy and needed something to keep me awake. Seiko, who was deathly tired, finally followed, because—as she later put it—she didn't want to die alone, and within a few hours we came right out at the monastery again. It was early evening, and the others hadn't even noticed we were gone.

Given my predilection for mountains, I will doubtless have trouble with snow again, but re-

garding Zen haiku, nowadays I prefer a lighter
kind of poem.

> man in a blanket—
> looking as though the snowflakes
> have made him smaller

• Try This •

Go someplace outdoors where you can be alone
without being disturbed. Carry your notebook, but
make no effort to write a poem.

- Allow yourself to be the way you are.
Offer no resistance to what is happening inside you, whatever that might be.
If you're sad, be sad. If sleepy, then
allow yourself to doze. If nothing in
particular seems to be on your mind,
then allow your mind to wander in a
nothing-in-particular kind of way.

- Do not try to notice anything special
in nature, but leave the things of nature as they are. If that seems too difficult, then imagine them going on
without you. Imagine yourself unnec-

essary to the scene, and see what happens with you not there.

• Don't give in to boredom if nothing happens. And don't give in to the impulse to write a poem. Continue in this poem-less place for twenty or thirty minutes, and then return home.

If you try this practice (and it becomes more difficult the longer you write haiku—until much later, when it becomes easy again), you will find that, sometime afterwards, you are able to write a haiku that surpasses anything you are normally able to achieve.

This exercise is based on a paradox: if you become too attached to haiku, you will not be able to write haiku. When you give up haiku, you'll be able to write haiku once again. Do this practice more often if you find your haiku are getting stale.

Faith

There is a strong element of faith that enters into the composition of a poem. Particularly in haiku, where the poet tends to allow a moment to speak for itself, faith is the one essential precondition. But faith in what, or whom? There are many ways of saying it: the spontaneous creative principle of nature, always full, complete, and perfect as it is. Or faith in one's own intuition and the ability to express it in words. One might even extend that faith to include the reader, whom we trust to intuit the heart of the poem.

I have found that I no longer have much interest in the origins of faith. Nowadays I prefer simply to let it function. Even as I write these words, I have glanced up from my desk to see

sparrows flutter down
into bushes full of light
without any leaves

March

March in the garden—
my hostess shows me brown sticks
and speaks of flowers

—Sister Benedicta

Two women standing before a garden not
yet in flower. Only some of the brown stems remain from the year before. Because it is her garden, however, the hostess is able to explain where

each type of flower will bloom. Earlier I told the story of how a friend of mine once handed me an empty cup and, as a kind of joke, said, "Zen tea."

When I read this poem, I imagine the women as somewhat older, and it is hard for me to believe that each of them has not been involved with spiritual practice for many years. Everything about the poem seems to point to that conclusion. This is real Zen tea.

Grass

trembling from the weight
the wet grass pokes its way up
from between the stones

(submitted anonymously at a
workshop in the mountains)

Grass is both the strongest and the weakest thing. On the one hand, it cracks abandoned highways and forces the mortar out from between stones. On the other, its blades are easily broken just by walking through a field.

It is easy to imagine what must have happened. The poet caught sight of a grass stalk trembling with beads of water. Perhaps she had brushed it with her boot. Noticing that the grass had forced its way up from between the mountain stones, briefly it seemed to her that the grass stalk must be trembling from the weight of the stones— a momentary misperception which, nevertheless, captures the spirit of grass.

The turn of thought lies somewhere in between the words "trembling" and "poke," triggering the sudden recognition that the grass is strong, yet gentle—both at once.

The Second- Class Art

Haiku is enormously popular in Japan. A recent book estimates that there are as many as six million people actively composing haiku in Japan. The popularity of the form lies partly in its accessibility and social value: a haiku can be composed easily in a moment or two and shared with someone on the spot. In this way, they may be used to show appreciation or to commemorate a particular event or gathering, or to capture a special feeling one has shared with another.

Many social gatherings are centered around haiku. All over Japan, groups of local poets meet once a month to discuss their poems, and once each season the group goes on a *ginko* (poetry walk) to some beautiful or historic place for the purpose of writing haiku on the spot.

And haiku are ubiquitous. Most major newspapers carry a haiku column at least once a week—sometimes on the front page—and one finds haiku printed on hand towels and other common everyday items. Some haiku are so strongly associated with a particular place that they are carved—often in the poet's own calligraphy—on large natural stones for permanent public view. These "haiku stones" commemorate the work of great masters and are truly numberless throughout Japan.

For these very reasons perhaps, in this century haiku has been called a second-class art—an amateur pastime practiced by too many people to be taken seriously as a literary art (an idea which rests upon the belief that poetry by its nature must remain essentially an elitist practice).

In 1946 Kuwabara Takeo of Kyoto University published what was to become a famous essay.

Its title was "Second-Class Art." Kuwabara's basic premise was that twentieth-century haiku lacked objective standards, failed to address the issues of modern life, and consequently had become an amateur pastime rather than a serious literary art. Naturally, haiku masters of the day were outraged at Kuwabara's claim. According to Donald Keene, "Some haiku masters wrote strong retorts, but Kyoshi accepted the judgment with the ironic remark that he was pleased that haiku had been promoted to being second class!"

Takahama Kyoshi, one of Shiki's two most gifted students, was by then the most famous haiku master in Japan. Editor of the magazine *Hototogisu,* he had been influential in establishing the reputations of nearly every major poet of the day. Indeed, it was largely Kyoshi's efforts in working with beginners that made haiku so enormously popular in this century.

Nevertheless, on this occasion, Kyoshi seemed to indicate that haiku was less than second class. How could this be so? Why would anyone who loved haiku ever say such a thing. It seemed to contradict everything Kyoshi stood for. And yet, the truth is, with that comment Kyoshi set himself apart from the other haiku masters of his day as a man of true understanding.

The lesson of the second-class art is exceptionally difficult to learn. I have found that even when students have come to some understanding of it intellectually, they fail to actually produce it on the spot. Nearly always there is some neurotic striving, some inability to let things be. I have even been offered the excuse that this is part of the poetic temperament, but I do not believe that this is so. At least I can say with confidence that it is not true of haiku. It is not necessary to be neurotic in order to write them. Still, of the many poets writing haiku in English today, I know of almost no one who, if told that haiku were second class would know to reply, "Thank you, but no—not even second class."

Deh Chun

I never had the privilege of studying with Takahama Kyoshi, who died when I was only two years old. However, I had a teacher who in one crucial respect was just the same.

My first Zen teacher was an elderly Ch'an Buddhist monk living out his retirement a few miles from the town where I attended college. It seems improbable to me now that a Ch'an monk should have been living in Monteagle, Tennessee, but with the innocence of youth I simply accepted the fact when I heard it and went to see him. I was nineteen.

Deh Chun's small house was chock full of odds and ends, and everything in it was made from the cheapest possible materials: plywood, two-by-fours, the piece of foam on which he slept. One room was heated by a small two-burner wood stove, about ankle-high, upon which he also cooked all of his food. Everything he owned looked as though it might have been pulled directly out of other people's garbage.

He was very small and frail looking. What I remember most about his appearance was how, even with his few remaining teeth, he just smiled anyway. His clothes were all purchased at the local Goodwill store without any regard to style or era, though I seem to recall he preferred earth tone colors. As I write these words, it occurs to me for the first time that they were the clothes of old men who had lived out their lives and died in Monteagle, Tennessee.

He must have shaved his head with some regularity, for his hair was always a very short gray stubble, but I cannot now recall ever having seen his head completely bald. Several years ago

I lost my only photograph of him, a badly exe-
cuted Instamatic shot, too dark to see much of
anything but his face and diminutive body
dwarfed by a door frame. I am now certain I
would never have given him a second look had I
not been told by my art history professor that he
was a Ch'an Buddhist monk and probably the very
last of a line of Zen recluses still painting in the
old Chinese style.

I once asked him how he made such beautiful paintings, and he replied by asking me how
I drove a car. We had just returned from a drive
around the mountains, so I thought he might just
be putting me off. But he insisted that I *show* him,
so finally I mimicked the movements of driving,
turning this way and that, now and then reaching
down with one hand to shift the gears. When I
had finished, he mimed the movements of painting something like a tree limb, following a line
this way and that, every few moments returning
to an imaginary inkwell to dip his imaginary
brush.

This was the way he always taught. He
never spoke of Buddhism or Zen. He lived on fifty
dollars a month, didn't have a phone, and never

used more than the minimum charge for electricity. He gardened all year around, somehow managing to extract vegetables from the ground underneath a thick clear plastic sheet even in the dead of winter.

Though he was a strict vegetarian and would not even use honey to sweeten his food, preferring molasses instead, I noticed that whenever I took him out for a meal at one of the local greasy spoons, he would happily accept anything I offered short of meat. He seemed concerned that I did not eat properly and insisted that I ought to think about that before I started getting any big ideas about Buddhism. I had no idea what he meant. I just thought of him as some kind of fanatical vegetarian and avoided discussions of food whenever I possibly could.

My friend Michael and I had a hard time with him at the University. He seemed to lose his manners and become completely uncouth the moment we brought him into contact with other people. He would purchase a huge bag of potato chips, empty them over the surface of a table, and invite anyone who passed, including our professors, to share them with us. Whenever we passed a beautiful girl on the sidewalk, he would cover one nostril and blow snot out of the other at her feet. We once had him over for dinner because a certain religion professor, a specialist in hermeneutics, had wanted to meet him. He arrived somewhat better dressed than usual, wearing a secondhand wool sports coat, became drunk on a thimbleful of wine and chattered all night long about the communists in China, seeming not to understand any of the questions he was asked.

When my first wife and I were married, however, we received a beautiful card copied out in copperplate script "regretfully declining the kind invitation to your wedding celebration of May the twenty-sixth" and wishing us a long and happy life together. Once, when we visited him after that, my wife was so overcome with affection that she leaned over suddenly and kissed him on the face. I remember that he blushed but did not pull away. After that, she received a number of plain white U.S. postal cards partially covered over with Chinese mountain landscapes drawn in blue ballpoint pen.

When I left the monkhood in 1990, my Japanese Zen teacher told me that a student never fully appreciates his teacher until they have been separated for at least ten years. This lesson was brought home to me in a powerful way last year by circumstances which were, however, altogether ordinary.

I had returned to Sewanee, Tennessee, for my youngest sister's graduation. I had not been back in many years. With me I brought my second wife, Perdita, at that time four months pregnant with our daughter. There were many places I wanted to show her, but Deh Chun's house was the most important of all. It seemed that everything had taken place within its walls. But after searching every street in Monteagle, the house was nowhere to be found. Later, prompted by my declaration that the house was no longer there, Michael flew from Berkeley to see for himself and, of course, found it just where it had always been, looking slightly better kept, as a home for a woman and her son. Perdita said she thought I didn't want to see the house again, and perhaps she is right.

In any event, at the time I felt dejected. In a kind of daze I allowed myself to be led into the local grocery store, where I stood around feeling lost while Perdita looked for vegetables to make a salad. Soon a very large man approached me and began to talk about my sandals, their make and design, a similar pair he had owned just last year, and the pair his brother had bought last spring. He frightened me a little. He wore a crewcut, army fatigues, and a T-shirt, and he seemed a little unhinged. But after a moment I realized that he was friendly after all. Only, he was mildly retarded.

So I relaxed and we spoke about sandals and footwear in general, and I noticed that his hair looked unusually soft, like Deh Chun's had looked.

One never knows why certain events seem so much more powerful than others, why for instance a funeral affects one less than a watch taken from a drawer after many years, but as I was pulling out of the parking lot I had to stop the car. After a moment, I started up once more, but had to stop again. Finally I just wept. And the thought that kept going over and over in my mind was that Deh Chun's teachings had left nothing out. They had been so unremarkable and plain I hadn't noticed them at all.

Failure

and

Disappointment

Think of it this way. In the beginning we understand a haiku to be only a seventeen-syllable poem. Later we find out more. There are certain principles that need to be mastered before we are proficient at the art. There is a discipline to take up and perfect. But the perfection of that discipline turns out to be a bust, and the principles we worked so hard to perfect are just the same—which is a great letdown, because we had become very invested in what we could do.

This very disappointment is the beginning of true mastery. Ultimately the ego cannot reach beyond itself with all of its perfected technique. However, the Way of Haiku will not emerge until it has been offered up.

I once heard haiku described as a perfectly transparent window on the world. A few years later I came across a poet who suggested that the window was open so that it was possible to look at things directly, rather than through glass. Nowadays I would say that the perfection of haiku comes only when the house has been abandoned for the out-of-doors.

the white butterfly
disappears in a sun shaft
on the rocky trail

The
Superficial
Art

Haiku is a shallow art. I sometimes begin a workshop with those words. I find they somehow set people at ease. Almost always, some people have come fully expecting to write a Zen poem, while others fear that even their best effort will be rejected. So the overturning of expectations all around has the effect of bringing people back to where they are. Which is a good place to begin writing haiku.

I ought to explain, however, that the word

shallow—at least when applied to haiku—does not mean lacking depth. Rather, it means that in haiku we find meaning in what lies right before the eye. We don't look past the thing itself for something else. This is really just another way of saying that haiku leaves the mind and the objects of nature in their natural state. It does not make them into ideas, nor does it make them subject to attachment or aversion. It also means that the haiku mind is like a mirror.

We sometimes notice when we read classical Japanese haiku—and especially those of Bashō or Issa—that they often choose as their subjects things which are more ordinary than beautiful, and at times even slightly distasteful or repugnant to our ordinary way of thinking. On his celebrated journey to the far north, Bashō writes about being bitten by lice and fleas, and the sound of a horse pissing next to his pillow. At another time he writes of sea slugs all frozen together in one lump; and at still another, of a warbler's droppings fallen on a rice cake at the end of a verandah. Issa writes about shitting and about pissing in the snow.

And yet, in all of these haiku the principal point—in which each poet takes a kind of secret joy—lies in the fact that each of these things arises directly from the Haiku Mind. They are not separate from it, they are its natural expression, even as they may bring a grimace or a smile to the poet's face and the reader's in turn. And, of course, haiku such as these point to a profound spiritual truth where beauty is concerned: namely, that it is more useful, and more spiritually nourishing, to find beauty in what is ordinary and close at hand, than to invent it solely from the mind, in accordance with some predetermined code of values—and especially a code that sets one thing against another as being lovely on the one hand, or detestable on the other.

The wisdom of haiku, then, comes not so much from keeping to the surface of the moment, since that is impossible by ordinary reckoning— for thoughts and feelings naturally arise—but from recognizing whatever rises as the activity of, and not contrary to or separate from, the ground of being.

So, when I speak of haiku as a superficial art, the surface I speak of is really just the ground of being. It is the Haiku Mind.

a fingernail moon:
all that is left in the sky
after the blizzard

—Perdita Finn

the weathervane points
at the buds of cherry trees
pink and opening

—Perdita Finn

an April shower
turning the meadow greener
than it was before

—Dennis Davidson

repainting the house
yellow covering yellow
in September light

       –Susan Rudnick

when I walk away
the wet logs finally burn
in the cabin stove

       –Susan Rudnick

The
Rose
in the
Vase

The following poem was written by a high school student in New Jersey last year after a brief introduction to haiku:

The rose in the vase
It still blooms even though it's
broken from the rest

—Jane Song

The season is summer. A single rose has been broken from the bush outside and placed in a vase of water on the table, where it blooms.

It would be nearly impossible for someone who had studied haiku for a few years to compose a poem of this quality. Such haiku come only at the beginning or after many years. This is why it is sometimes said that haiku is a form best suited to children and to accomplished masters of the art. This is also the reason that established poets often have so much trouble with haiku, the reason why—far more often than not—they write bad haiku. They cannot understand that the greatest haiku are artless and uncontrived.

In the beginning we see things clearly. On the one hand, we know very little and may find it difficult to tell good haiku from bad. On the other, we have fewer ideas to come between us and the poem. As time goes on, however, and we learn more about haiku, we tend to lose this fresh "beginner's mind." We become too interested in being clever or profound. Unfortunately, as a re sult of this attitude, our haiku only become predictable and stale. They begin to have a tainted look, as though they had been handled too much in the making.

The Way of Haiku begins to emerge when, having mastered the subtleties of the art, one "forgets" them, becoming like a beginner again. To be sure, there is a difference. Having cultivated a deep understanding of haiku over many years of practice in contemplating nature, the master can afford to forget it all and just work naturally from the heart. This is because his understanding has *become* his heart. When he composes a haiku, there is no separation at all.

Bashō's
Last
Words

It is one thing to say that the proper concern of haiku is the things of nature, and quite another to really practice that. Even among those who practice it, it is quite another thing to follow it to the end.

A story told of Bashō says that on the last day of his life he mostly slept, but awoke around noon to notice that many flies had gathered on the sliding screen. His students were taking turns trying to catch them with a lime stick. When Bashō saw this he only laughed and said, "Those flies seem delighted to have a sick man around unexpectedly."

A Violet

When the master considers a violet, he for-gets himself before a violet and a violet marks the Way.

When a violet marks the Way, it bears the master's mark.

That mark is no other than a violet. A violet *is* the master's mark.

Recommended Reading

Aitken, Robert. *A Zen Wave: Bashō's Haiku and Zen*. New York: Weatherhill, 1978.

Beichman, Janine. *Masaoka Shiki*. New York: Kodansha, 1986.

Blyth, R. H. *Haiku*. 4 vols. Tokyo: Hokuseido Press, 1949–52.

Hamill, Sam. *Narrow Road to the Interior*. Boston: Shambhala, 1991.

Hass, Robert. *The Essential Haiku: Versions of Bashō, Buson, and Issa*. Hopewell, New Jersey: Ecco, 1994.

Henderson, Harold G. *An Introduction to Haiku*. New York: Doubleday, 1958.

Higginson, William J. *The Haiku Handbook: How to Write, Share, and Teach Haiku*. New York: Kodansha, 1992.

———. *The Haiku Seasons: Poetry of the Natural World*. New York: Kodansha, 1996.

Kametaro, Yagi. *Haiku: Messages from Matsuyama*. Edited by Oliver Statler. Santa Fe, New Mexico: Katydid Books, 1991.

Keene, Donald. *Dawn to the West: Japanese Literature in the*

Modern Era, Poetry, Drama, Criticism. New York: Henry Holt, 1984.

Nakagawa, Soen. *Endless Vow: The Zen Path of Soen Nakagawa.* Compiled and Translated by Kazuaki Tanahashi & Roko Sheri Chayat. Boston: Shambhala, 1996.

Sato, Hiroaki. *One Hundred Frogs: From Renga to Haiku in English.* New York: Weatherhill, 1983.

Sen, Soshitsu. *Tea Life, Tea Mind.* New York and Tokyo: Weatherhill, 1979.

Suzuki, Shunryu. *Zen Mind, Beginner's Mind.* New York and Tokyo: Weatherhill, 1970.

Ueda, Makoto. *Matsuo Bashō.* New York: Kodansha, 1970.

Yamaguchi, Seishi. *The Essence of Modern Haiku: 300 Poems by Seishi Yamaguchi.* Trans. by Takashi Kodaira and Alfred H. Marks. Atlanta: Mangajin, 1993.

Yasuda, Kenneth. *The Japanese Haiku: Its Essential Nature, History, and Possibilities in English.* Tokyo: Tuttle, 1958.

• About the Author •

Clark Strand has been an English teacher, a Zen Buddhist monk, and, most recently, Senior Editor of *Tricyle: The Buddhist Review*. He has been writing haiku for over twenty years and is the founder of New York Haiku-kai, a traditional English language haiku group. He lives in the Catskill Mountains with his wife and two children.